W0007170
9781898838074

Alpha
Cookbook

First published 1996
Reprinted June 1997
New edition June 1999

Published by HTB Publications with Alpha Resources
Holy Trinity Brompton, Brompton Road
London, SW7 1JA

Illustrations by Charlie Mackesy

Printed in the UK by TPS print
Exhibition House, 6 Warren Lane, London, SE18 6BW

Contents

Foreword

Food has always been an important part of the Alpha course. It provides the setting in which people get to know each other and form lasting friendships. Alpha is a 15-session practical introduction to the Christian faith. Our own course has grown to over 500 attending each session. Each evening the programme includes supper together, a talk about such subjects as 'Who is Jesus?' and 'Why did Jesus die?' followed by discussion groups.

At first, when the course was very small, catering was easy; people simply took turns cooking. As the course grew to about 120, small groups would cook on a rota basis. However, when the numbers reached 250 it no longer seemed fair to ask anyone to make shepherd's pie for so many people! So we decided to call in a professional - Harriet Lanyon, who kindly came to the rescue.

Harriet's past experience in creating delicious yet economical food for large groups ensured that her cooking was a huge success with young and old alike, so much so that many churches have been requesting the recipes. I am absolutely thrilled that she has now agreed to make the recipes available for everyone.

I sometimes say that I would like the food on Alpha to have such a good reputation that, if for nothing else, people would come simply for that. Harriet's recipes make this a real possibility.

Nicky Gumbel
Holy Trinity Brompton

Cooking for Alpha

Over the years we have found that a simple but filling meal at the start of the session helps people relax, stimulates conversation and also does wonders for encouraging people to turn up on time!

It does not have to be a five course banquet! Alpha budgets are always tight, but with a little imagination, some stock recipes and a good group of helpers it's amazing what can be achieved.

The recipes in Section 2 are my favourite - quick and easy to prepare but always popular with people on the course. Group sizes vary, so I have provided quantity guidelines which you can adapt to your numbers.

In Section 3 I have included a selection of menus for Alpha 'parties' which many groups hold as an 'end-of-course celebration' to which friends and family can be invited. To fit the occasion I keep the preparation simple but offer a more stylish menu. It must have worked well in the past - I am continually asked for the recipes!

You will of course have recipes of your own to add to these - but I hope they provide some ideas to get you started.

Have fun cooking for Alpha!

Harriet Lanyon

"Hate religion - love food"

Section 1 - Before you start

Good preparation is vital. There's nothing worse than finding yourself short of ingredients when you are halfway through a meal for 200! So make sure you have the right equipment, a comprehensive shopping list and a reliable band of helpers lined up.

1. Premises

Make sure that the premises you use have the necessary facilities to cope with the numbers involved! There is no point in making life difficult for yourself by cooking for large numbers at home if the church can have access to larger kitchen facilities.

Make sure, though, that any outside premises are spotlessly clean and, if used regularly, checked out by the local environmental health officer (EHO). Just because Alpha menus are simple, it doesn't mean you can dispense with the basic food safety and hygiene guidelines which ensure that a delicious meal in the evening is still remembered as such the following morning! If in doubt, ask your local EHO for a copy of the current guidelines.

If using public kitchens, don't forget to book them well ahead!

2. Equipment

If your group is small you will probably have the necessary equipment at home. If the numbers are large, however, you'll need to make sure that you have access to the following:

Large oven

Large fridge

Large saucepans

Large frying pan

Large deep sided roasting trays

Large baking trays

As large a colander as possible

Electric mixer and attachments (e.g. Kenwood)

Food processor and attachments (e.g. Magimix)

Large mixing bowls

Utensils - chopping boards, sharp knives, knife sharpener, scissors, tin opener, sieve, wooden spoons, balloon whisk, metal spoons, ladles, fish slice, potato masher, spatula, garlic crusher, potato peeler, cheese grater, pastry brush, rolling pin, lemon squeezer, measuring scales and a measuring jug, pepper mill and first aid kit.

Don't forget - aprons, tea towels, oven gloves, matches, tin foil, cling film, kitchen roll, rubbish bags, washing up liquid, rubber gloves, cloths, scourers and brillo pads.

3. Planning your menus

My golden rule is to keep the menu short and simple. With only a limited time for eating, there is no need to prepare a gourmet extravaganza!

The menus in this book are my typical Alpha menus, easy to prepare and tested on Alpha groups of all sizes. They include one main course dish each week, together with popular supporters such as garlic or herbed bread, and salad. To save time and to keep things simple in the kitchen, pudding is usually fruit or a yoghurt. Orange or lemon squash is served with the meal. A cup of coffee is always popular, but to fit in with the schedule for the evening it is often made available after the speaker has finished. In any large group these days you're sure to find some vegetarians, so a non-meat alternative is usually necessary. It is a good idea, though, to make it available 'on request' - otherwise the meat-eaters opt for the vegetarian dish and there isn't enough for the vegetarians!

4. How many am I cooking for?

Alpha courses come in all sizes - I think 700 is the record! But don't be daunted by large numbers. These menus are designed to take the stress out of cooking for Alpha, no matter how big the group.

However, as most Alpha courses have between 12 and 100 participants, when I refer in the book to 'large numbers', I tend to mean 'greater than 30'.

With large numbers you will need to be stricter (and generally more economical) with portion sizes, so make sure there is plenty to go round. Brief your helpers accordingly.

The Alpha cook's nightmare is when the numbers double on the day of the event. Equally, there can be a waste of food if the numbers are less than expected. Try to encourage the leaders to firm up on numbers as early as possible, to enable you to prepare properly.

5. Getting help

All too often one person tries to do all the preparation. It's not worth it - there are usually people around only too happy to help out, whether it is with shopping, cooking, laying up, serving, washing up or preparing coffee.

Make sure that you get help with all these tasks. Ideally use the same volunteers each week and appoint a team leader to save time explaining the jobs to new people.

Course participants are ideal helpers beforehand, but with large numbers it's best to ask for other volunteers to wash up and serve coffee. Best of all, have a separate team altogether. This allows those on the course to be in at the start of the session.

6. Shopping

All the ingredients listed in the recipes in this book are available in large supermarkets. However, if you are catering for over 50 it is well worth ordering food from the supermarket a few days before to ensure availability.

If you have access to a cash and carry card it is convenient being able to buy in bulk for large numbers, but it does not necessarily work out any cheaper.

See if your local butcher or greengrocer will give you a good price for a bulk order - they may even deliver it to your door as well!

Your shopping list will change according to the week's menu. But I find certain things are on every week:

Paper napkins

Firm paper plates

Plastic cups (and holders if you're serving coffee)

Plastic forks (if you can, use 'proper' forks)

Orange and lemon squash

Sugar

Milk

Fruit or yoghurts and plastic teaspoons

Salad ingredients

Bread and margarine or butter

7. Timing

It is important to serve the meal on time as there is a lot to pack into the evening. The more people you are cooking for, the more preparation and cooking time will be needed. Please bear in mind that the timings I have suggested for large numbers are estimates only, and will vary according to quantities chosen.

8. Money

Don't forget to keep the receipts from your shopping trips and make sure you are reimbursed as soon as possible. Larger courses can build up a substantial shopping bill!

My own experience is that you should not expect to spend more than £1.50 - £2.25 per head on shopping for Alpha each week. As a general rule the lower the number catered for, the higher the cost per head.

Section 2 - Suggested Alpha Course Menus

Week 1
Pasta with tomato and basil sauce
Served with garlic bread and salad

Week 2
Chilli con carne
Served with rice and salad
Vegetarian: Vegetable and bean
curry

Week 3
Sausages with honey and mustard
Served in baps with salad
Vegetarian: Onion and red pepper quiche

Week 4
Fish pie
Served with peas
Vegetarian: Mushroom and tomato pizza

Week 5
Pasta with blue cheese, petit pois and bacon sauce
Served with herbed bread and salad
Vegetarian: Pasta with blue cheese, petit pois and courgette sauce

Week 6
Tuna, tomato and cheese ricebake
Served with french bread and salad
Vegetarian: Vegetable risotto

Week 7
Shepherd's pie
Served with peas

Vegetarian: Courgette and aubergine lasagne
Week 8
Ham and broccoli bake
Served with french bread and salad
Vegetarian: Broccoli and potato bake

Week 9
Barbecued sausages
Served in baps with salad
Vegetarian: Stuffed peppers

Week 10
Pasta with ratatouille
Served with garlic bread and salad

Cooks tips

Where I have picked up helpful hints over the years which make life easier for the cook or produce even better results, I have included them under the heading of 'cooks tips'.

Here are just a few which are relevant to all the recipes:

1. Ingredients are given in both metric and imperial measures. Choose either to follow metric or imperial, but not both!

2. When eggs are listed, I have based the number on size 3 eggs.

3. When milk is listed, use 'full fat'.

4. When cheddar cheese is listed, use medium to strong.

5. When beef, chicken, fish or vegetable stock are listed, use stock cubes.

Week 1

Pasta with tomato and basil sauce
Served with garlic bread and salad

This recipe is ideal for the first week as the number of people to feed can be a little unpredictable. Reserve a little of the sauce and have an extra packet of pasta in case more people than anticipated turn up. If not, this sauce can simply be mixed into the remaining pasta being served.

1. Put the tinned tomatoes, butter, olive oil, tomato purée, and onion halves into a saucepan. Season with the sugar, salt and black pepper.

2. Bring slowly to the boil, stirring occasionally and turn down the heat to simmer uncovered for 40-50 minutes.

3. Discard the onion halves as well as you can and then liquidize the sauce in a blender. Stir in the basil and adjust the seasoning if necessary. Re-heat the sauce.

4. Cook the pasta and once it has been cooked and drained, pour over the hot sauce and mix well.

5. Serve immediately with grated cheese.

 ## Cook's tips

If you have time, allow the basil to infuse by allowing the sauce to sit for 30 minutes before serving.

For large numbers: removing the onion can be a messy job. I would recommend allowing the sauce to cool a little before doing so. Do not worry about discarding all the onion, liquidizing the sauce will help! I would also advise keeping back a little of the sauce to help to 'loosen' the pasta when it starts to stick together during serving.

Ingredients	Quantities for 12	Quantities for 30	Quantities for 100
tinned tomatoes	3 x 400 g 3 x 14 oz	3 x 800 g 3 x 28 oz	10 x 800 g 10 x 28 oz
butter	170 g 6oz	340 g 12oz	1.15 kg 2 1/2 lb
olive oil	230 ml 8 floz	425 ml 3/4 pt	1.4lt 2 1/2 pt
tomato purée	140 g 5 oz	280 g 10 oz	900 g 2 lb
onions	450 g 1 lb	900 g 2 lb	2 1/2 kg 5 1/2 lb
sugar	1 tsp	2 tsp	2 tbsp
dried basil	1 1/2 tbsp	3 tbsp	20 g 3/4 oz
pasta	900 g 2 lb	1.8 kg 4 lb	5.9 kg 13 lb
cheddar cheese	225 g 8 oz	560 g 1 1/4 lb	1.8 kg 4 lb
salt & pepper	to taste	to taste	to taste

Week 2

Chilli con carne
Serve with rice and salad

YOU WILL NEED::

dried red kidney beans
(soaked overnight - max 12 hours -
in plenty of cold water)
oil
onions - peeled and chopped
garlic - crushed
minced beef
hot chilli powder
plain flour
cumin
dried oregano
salt and black pepper
tinned tomatoes
tomato purée
beef stock
long grain rice (see notes page 49)

1. Drain the beans, rinse, then put them into a large saucepan with enough water to cover. Bring to the boil and boil rapidly for 10-15 minutes. Drain the beans and then transfer them into a second pan of boiling water. Return to the boil, and reduce the heat to simmer gently for about 25-30 minutes until tender. Once cooked, drain and run under cold water until cold. Set aside.

2. Heat the oil in another saucepan and add the onions. Cook gently until soft, adding more oil if the onions start sticking to the bottom of the pan. Then stir in the garlic.

3. Add the mince and cook until it has browned, stirring all the time to break up the mince.

4. Add the chilli powder, plain flour, cumin and oregano. Season with salt and black pepper.

5. Stir in the tinned tomatoes, tomato purée and beef stock. Add more stock if the liquid does not quite cover the top of the mince. Bring to the boil.

6. Lower the heat so the mince simmers gently for 45 minutes (allow up to 2 hours if cooking a large quantity), stirring occasionally.

Add more stock if the mince is looking rather dry. Stir in the beans 30 minutes before the end of the cooking time.

7. Adjust the seasoning according to taste, reserving some of the liquid if the mince is looking too runny. Serve with the rice. (Cooking tip page 49)

Cook's tips

If you would like the chilli con carne hotter add a little more chilli powder when adjusting the seasonings, but be very careful not to use too much!

For large numbers: use a magimix or food processor to chop the onions. The onions will need to be roughly chopped first and then be careful not to 'overload' the machine with the onions or 'over chop' them.

Ingredients	Quantities for 12	Quantities for 30	Quantities for 100
dried red kidney beans	280 g 10 oz	675 g 1 1/2 lb	2.3 kg 5 lb
oil	3 tbsp	7 tbsp	290 ml 1/2 pt
oinions	3 large	1.35 kg 3 lb	4 1/2 kg 10 lb
garlic	2 cloves	4 cloves	1 head
minced beef	1 kg 2 1/4 lb	2 1/2 kg 5 1/2 lb	8.2 kg 18 lb
hot chilli powder	1 1/2 level tsp	3 3/4 level tsp	4 level tbsp
plain flour	1 tbsp	70 g 2 1/2 oz	225 g 8 oz
cumin	1/2 tbsp	1 1/2 tbsp	15 g 1/2 oz
dried oregano	1/2 tbsp	1 1/2 tbsp	15 g 1/2 oz
salt & pepper	to taste	to taste	to taste
tinned tomatoes	1 x 800 g 28 oz	2 x 800 g 28 oz	6 x 800 g 28 oz
tomato purée	3 tbsp	340 g 12 oz	1.15 kg 2.4 lb
beef stock (approx)	200 ml 7 floz	290 ml 1/2 pt	850 ml 1 1/2 pt
rice	675 g 1 1/2 lb	1 1/2 kg 3 1/4 lb	4.8 kg 10 1/2 lb

Week 3

Sausages in honey and mustard
Serve in baps with salad

This is very popluar and is the quickest recipe to prepare, two very good reasons for including sausages twice among my Alpha menus (see week 9, Barbecued Sausages, page 33).

YOU WILL NEED:

oil
sausages (large - e.g. 8 sausages to 450 g (1 lb))
clear honey
grain mustard
salt and black pepper
baps - sliced almost in half

1. Preheat the oven to 200 C/ 400 F/ gas mark 6.

2. Pour some oil to cover the base of one or two roasting trays. Line up the sausages in the trays but do not 'overcrowd' them or it will be difficult to turn the sausages.

3. Cook the sausages in the oven, turning them over once one side has browned. When the sausages are cooked, loosen them from the base of the trays and tip off the oil. Set aside. If you have more sausages to cook repeat the above.

4. Put the honey and mustard into a saucepan together and stir over a medium heat. Season with salt and black pepper. Once the sauce has come almost to the boil, turn off the heat.

"tell me how to become a Christian."

5. Pile the sausages into one or two roasting trays and pour over the hot sauce, tossing the sausages so they are well coated. Cover the trays with tin foil and return to the oven to re-heat the sausages.

6. Serve piping hot with two sausages in the centre of each bap.

Cook's tip

For large numbers: do not forget to order the baps from your supermarket and, if necessary, the sausages.

Ingredients	Quantities for 12	Quantities for 30	Quantities for 100
oil (approx)	3 tbsp	7tbsp	290 ml 1/2 pt
large sausages	1.35 kg 3 lb	3.4 kg 7 1/2 lb	11.35 kg 25 lb
clear honey	340 g 12 oz	800 g 1 3/4 lb	2.7 kg 6 lb
grain mustard	340 g 12 oz	800 g 1 3/4 lb	2.7 kg 6 lb
salt & pepper	to taste	to taste	to taste
baps	12	30	100

Week 4

Fish pie
Serve with peas

YOU WILL NEED:

cod fillets
smoked haddock fillets
milk
onions - peeled and sliced
bay leaves
peppercorns
eggs - hard-boiled and cut into eight
margarine
plain flour
salt and black pepper
potatoes - peeled and cut in half if large
milk - for the potatoes
margarine or butter - for the potatoes
peas

1. Preheat the oven to 180°C/ 350°F/ gas mark 4.

2. Lay the fish fillets (skin side up) into several roasting trays. Heat the milk in a saucepan and pour over the fish, dividing the onions, bay leaves and peppercorns between the roasting trays. Cover with tin foil and place in the oven.

3. Cook the fish for 15 minutes until the fish is firm and opaque in colour. Remove the fillets from the milk and spread them out on to large trays to cool slightly. Strain off   the milk, reserving it for the sauce.

4. In a bowl, flake the fish into large pieces, removing the skin and bones. This is easier to do while the fish is still warm.

Add the eggs and set aside.

5. Make the sauce by melting the margarine in a large saucepan over a medium heat. Stir in the flour and cook for one minute, stirring all the time. Take the pan off the heat and add the reserved milk. Mix well with a balloon whisk.

6. Return to the heat and stir constantly with the whisk until the sauce has thickened and come to the boil. Turn down the heat and allow the sauce to cook for a further 2 minutes. Be very careful not to let the sauce catch on the bottom of the pan. Season with salt and black pepper.

7. With a wooden spoon stir in the flaked fish and eggs. Then, tip the mixture carefully into a large pie dish or deep sided roasting trays.

8. Cook the potatoes by bringing them to the boil in a saucepan of salted water and turn down the heat to cook the potatoes gently (if you have an enormous pan of potatoes it could take over 50 minutes to come to the boil). Once cooked, drain through a colander and mash with the milk and margarine or butter. Season with salt and black pepper.

9. Spread the mashed potato evenly on top of the fish mixture. Make a pattern with a fork on the potato and place the pies in the oven for about 20 minutes or longer (up to about 45 minutes if they are large).

10. Serve with peas tossed in a little butter.

Cook's tips

For large numbers: to save time, if you have a good greengrocer they may be able to supply you with potatoes that are already peeled or failing this you could make up 'packet' mashed potato. Use your food mixer to mash the potatoes but you may find you use less milk.

Ingredients	Quantities for 12	Quantities for 30	Quantities for 100
cod fillets	1.35 kg 3 lb	3.2 kg 7 lb	10.9 kg 24 lb
smoked haddock fillets	450 g 1 lb	1.15 kg 2 1/2 lb	3.6 kg 8 lb
milk	850ml 1 1/2 pt	2lt 3 1/2 pt	6.8lt 12 pt
onions	1 large	3	1.6 kg 3 1/2 lb
bay leaves	2	5	16
peppercorns	1/4 tsp	1/2 tsp	2 tsp
eggs	6	15	48
margarine	70 g 2 1/2 oz	155 g 5 1/2 oz	510 g 1 lb 2 oz
plain flour	70 g 2 1/2 oz	155 g 5 1/2 oz	510 g 1 lb 2 oz
salt & pepper	to taste		
potatoes	1.8 kg 4 lb	4 1/2 kg 10 lb	15 kg 33 lb
milk (for the potatoes)	115 ml 4 fl oz	290 ml 1/2 pt	850 ml 1 1/2 pt
margarine/butter (for the potatoes)	45 g 1 1/2 oz	110 g 4 oz	340 g 12 oz
peas	900 g 2 lb	2.05 kg 4 1/2 lb	6.3 kg 14 lb

Week 5

Pasta with blue cheese, petit pois & bacon
Served with herbed bread and salad

YOU WILL NEED:

petit pois
oil
bacon- dice, removing the
rind and any gristle
or gammon - prepare as above
margarine
plain flour
milk
stilton cheese - grated or crumbled
salt and black pepper
pasta (see notes page 48)
oil (preferably olive oil) - to toss
over the pasta

1. Bring the saucepan of water to the boil and tip in the petit pois. Once the water has come back to the boil, drain immediately through a colander and run under cold water until the petit pois are cold. Set aside.

2. Heat some of the oil in a frying pan and fry the bacon in batches. Put the bacon once cooked onto the kitchen paper to absorb the fat. Repeat until all the bacon is cooked and set aside.

3. Make the cheese sauce by melting the margarine in a large saucepan over a medium heat. Stir in the flour and cook for one minute, stirring all the time. Take the pan off the heat and add the milk. Mix well with a balloon whisk.

4. Return to the heat and stir constantly with the whisk until the sauce has thickened and come to the boil. Turn down the heat and allow the sauce to cook for a further 2 minutes. Be very careful not to let the sauce catch on the bottom of the pan.

5. Add all the cheese and mix well. Do not allow the sauce to boil now that the cheese has been added.

6. Add the petit pois and bacon*. Season the sauce with salt and black pepper but check how 'salty' the sauce is before adding the salt (the cheese and bacon are salty flavours).

7. Cook the pasta and once it has been drained, toss the pasta generously in oil (to help prevent it sticking together).

8. Serve a portion of pasta with a ladle of hot sauce on top.

Cook's tips

For large numbers: ask your butcher to prepare the bacon for you but make sure to ask for small dice and the fat removed. You may prefer to use diced, cooked ham rather than frying a large amount of bacon.

Bring the milk almost to the boil in a separate saucepan before making the sauce. It is quicker and there is less chance of it catching on the bottom of the saucepan while making the sauce.

*For each vegetarian remove a ladle of sauce and add 30g (1oz) fried, diced courgette per person instead of bacon.

Ingredients	Quantities for 12	Quantities for 30	Quantities for 100
petit pois	340 g 12 oz	675 g 1 1/2 lb	2.3 g 5 lb
oil	2 tbsp	4 tbsp	170 ml 6 fl oz
bacon or gammon	450 g 1 lb	900 g 2 lb	3 kg 6 1/2 lb
margarine	85 g 3 oz	170 g 6 oz	560 g 1 1/4 lb
plain flour	85 g 3 oz	170 g 6 oz	560 g 1 1/4 lb
milk	1.15 ml 2 pt	2.3 ml 4 pt	7.4 lt 13 pt
stilton cheese	255 g 9 oz	510 g 1 lb 2 oz	1.8 kg 4 lb
salt & pepper	to taste	to taste	to taste
pasta	900 g 2 lb	1.8 kg 4 lb	5.9 kg 13 lb
olive oil			

Week 6

Tuna, tomato and cheese ricebake
Serve with french bread and salad

YOU WILL NEED:

oil
onions - peeled and sliced
tinned tuna
long grain rice
(see notes page 49)
tinned tomatoes
dried basil
dried oregano
salt and black pepper
cheddar cheese -grated
mozzarella cheese - grated
fish stock

1. Preheat the oven to 200°C/ 400°F/ gas mark 6.

2. Heat the oil in a saucepan and add the onions, cooking them gently until they are soft but not coloured. Add more oil if the onions start sticking to the bottom of the pan. Drain   off any liquid and set aside.

3. Mix together the tuna, rice, tinned tomatoes and herbs in a bowl. Season generously with salt and black pepper. Add the onions and stir well. In a separate bowl mix the two cheeses together.

4. Grease a large pie dish or deep sided roasting trays and layer up the rice mixture alternatively with the cheese, starting with the rice mixture and finishing with the cheese.

5. Pour over enough hot fish stock to reach just above the surface of the mixture.

6. Cook in the oven for approximately 45 minutes (up to 1 1/2 hours if the trays are very large). The bake is cooked when the rice is 'al dente' to the bite, not too firm or soft. Check the bake regularly as it

may need covering with tin foil if it is going too brown on top. It may also be necessary to add more fish stock if it is looking too dry.

The ricebake should be juicy but not too wet. If it looks too wet, drain off the excess liquid and allow the ricebake to sit in the oven until the remaining liquid has been absorbed.

Cook's tip

Buy mozzarella ready grated if you are doing a lot as it's not easy to grate, even in a magimix!

Ingredients	Quantities for 12	Quantities for 30	Quantities for 100
oil	2 tbsp	6 tbsp	290 ml 1/2 pt
onions	2 medium	900 g 2 lb	3 kg 6 1/2 lb
tinned tuna	675 g 1 1/2lb	1.7 kg 3 3/4 lb	5.6 kg 12 1/4 lb
long grain rice	400 g 14 oz	965 g 2 lb 2 oz	3.2 kg 7lb
tinned tomatoes	3 x 200g 3 x 7 oz	2 x 800g 2 x 28 oz	7 x 800g 7 x 28 oz
dried basil	1 tbsp	2 tbsp	20 g 3/4 oz
dried oregano	1 tbsp	2 tbsp	20 g 3/4 oz
salt & pepper	to taste	to taste	to taste
cheddar cheese	400 g 14 oz	900 g 2 lb	3 kg 6 1/2 lb
mozarella cheese	400 g 14 oz	900 g 2 lb	3 kg 6 1/2 lb
fish stock (approx)	570 ml 1 pt	1.4 lt 2 1/2 pt	41/2 lt 8 pt

Week 7

Shepherd's pie
Serve with peas

1. Preheat the oven to 220^0C/ 400^0F/ gas mark 6.

2. Heat the oil in a saucepan and add the chopped vegetables. Cook gently until soft, adding more oil if the vegetables start sticking to the bottom of the pan.

3. Add the mince and cook until browned, stirring all the time to break up the mince.

4. Stir in the flour and cook for a further minute. Then mix in the stock, tinned tomatoes and herbs. Add more stock if the liquid does not quite cover the top of the mince. Season with salt and black pepper.

5. Bring to the boil and then lower the heat to allow the mince to simmer gently for about 45 minutes (allow up to 2 hours if cooking a large quantity), stirring occasionally. Add more stock if the mince is looking rather dry.

6. Cook the potatoes by bringing them to the boil in a saucepan of salted water and turn down the heat to cook the potatoes gently (if

you have an enormous pan of potatoes it could take over 50 minutes to come to the boil). Once cooked, drain through a colander and mash with the milk and margarine or butter. Season with salt and black pepper.

7. Put the mince into a large pie dish or deep sided roasting trays, reserving some of the liquid if the mince is too runny. Spread the mashed potato evenly on top and make a pattern on the potato using a fork.

8. Bake in the oven for 25 minutes or longer (up to about 50 minutes) if you have made a large shepherd's pie. The potato should be golden brown and crusty on top.

9. Serve with peas tossed in a little butter.

Cook's tips

It is easier to spread the hot mashed potato on top of cold mince but remember to allow longer cooking time if you cook the shepherd's pie from cold.

For large numbers: use a magimix or food processor to chop the vegetables. They will need to be roughly chopped first and then be careful not to 'overload' the machine with the vegetables or 'over chop' them.

To save time, if you have a good greengrocer they may be able to supply you with potatoes which are already peeled or failing this you could make up 'packet' mashed potato. Use your food mixer to mash the potatoes, but you may find you use less milk.

Ingredients	Quantities for 12	Quantities for 30	Quantities for 100
oil	4 tbsp	10 tbsp	290 ml 1/2 pt
onions	2 medium	1 kg 2 1/4 lb	3.2 kg 7 lb
carrots	2	450 g 1 lb	1.6 kg 3 1/2 lb
celery	2 sticks	5 sticks	2 heads
minced beef	1.35 kg 3 lb	3.4 kg 7 1/2 lb	11.35 kg 25 lb
plain flour	1 1/2 tsp	110 g	340 g 12 oz
beef stock (approx)	290 ml 1/2 pt	850 ml 1 1/2 pt	2.3 lt 4 pt
tinned tomatoes	1 x 400 g 1 x 14 oz	1 x 800 g 1 x 28 oz	4 x 800 g 4 x 28 oz
dried mixed herbs	1 tbsp	2 1/2 tbsp	20g 3/4 oz
salt & pepper	to taste	to taste	to taste
potatoes	1.8 kg 4 lb	4 1/2 kg 10 lb	15 kg 33 lb
milk (approx)	115 ml 4 fl oz	290 ml 1/2 pt	850 ml 1 1/2 pt
margarine or butter	45 g 1 1/2 oz	110 g 4 oz	340 g 12 oz
peas	900 g 2 lb	2.05 kg 4 1/2 lb	6.3 kg 14 lb

Week 8

Ham and broccoli bake
Serve with french bread and salad

potatoes - peeled and cut in half if large
broccoli - chop off thick stems and cut into smaller sprigs
oil
onions - peeled and sliced
margarine
plain flour
milk
chicken stock
cheddar cheese - grated
gruyere cheese - grated
ham - diced
salt and black pepper

1. Preheat the oven to 200°C/ 400°F/ gas mark 6.

2. Put the potatoes into a large saucepan of cold, salted water. Bring to the boil and then lower the heat so the potatoes cook gently until they are firm but NOT SOFT (if you have an enormous saucepan of potatoes it could take over 50 minutes to come to the boil). Drain the potatoes through a colander and allow to go cold in a bowl of cold water, changing the water regularly as the cooling potatoes will warm the water. Once cooled, drain the potatoes and cut into thick slices. Set aside.

3. Bring another saucepan of salted water to the boil and add the broccoli. Cook until just tender but still quite firm. Drain and allow to go cold in a bowl of cold water, changing the water regularly as the broccoli cools. Once cooled, drain the broccoli and set aside.

4. Heat the oil in a clean saucepan and add the onions. Cook gently until soft but not coloured, adding more oil if the onions start sticking to the bottom of the pan. Drain off any liquid and set aside.

5. Make the sauce by melting the margarine in another saucepan over a medium heat. Stir in the flour and cook for one minute, stirring all the time. Take the pan off the heat and add the milk and the stock. Mix well with a balloon whisk.

6. Return to the heat and stir constantly with the whisk until the sauce has thickened and come to the boil. Turn down the heat and allow the sauce to cook for a further 2 minutes. Be very careful not to let the sauce catch on the bottom of the pan. Stir in the drained onions.

7. Mix the two cheeses together and add 170g (6oz) of cheese to every 570ml (1pt) of sauce and mix well. Do not allow the sauce to boil now the cheese has been added. Season with salt and black pepper.

8. Pour half the sauce into a large pie dish or deep sided roasting trays. Add a layer of potatoes, then a layer of ham and finally a layer of broccoli. Pour over the remaining sauce and sprinkle the rest of the cheese on top.

9. Cook in the oven for approximately 45 minutes (or up to 1 1/2 hours if you have made a very large bake). The bake should be hot and golden brown on top.

Cook's tips

Gruyere cheese is not cheap, so you may prefer to use more cheddar cheese and less gruyere cheese than in this recipe. Be careful not to break up the potatoes and broccoli when cooling them in cold water. For large numbers: watch out when cooking the broccoli, it is very easy to 'over cook'!

Bring the milk and stock almost to the boil in a separate pan before making the sauce. It is quicker and there is less chance of it catching on the bottom of the pan while making the sauce.
*For the vegetarian bake omit the ham.

Ingredients	Quantities for 12	Quantities for 30	Quantities for 100
potatoes	1.15 kg 2 1/2 lb	2.8 kg 6 1/4 lb	9 1/2 kg 21 lb
broccoli	900 g 2 lb	2.3 kg 5 lb	7 1/2 kg 16 1/2 lb
oil	2 1/2 tbsp	6 tbsp	290 ml 1/2 pt
onions	450 g 1 lb	1.15 kg 2 1/2 lb	3.9 kg 8 1/2 lb
margarine	55 g 2 oz	130 g 4 1/2 oz	425 g 15 oz
plain flour	55 g 2 oz	130 g 4 1/2 oz	425 g 15 oz
milk	425 ml 3/4 pt	850 ml 1 1/2 pt	2.8 lt 5 pt
chicken stock	425 ml 3/4 pt	850 ml 1 1/2 pt	2.8 lt 5 pt
salt & pepper	to taste		
cheddar cheese	280 g 10 oz	675 g 1 1/2 lb	2.3 kg 5 lb
gruyere cheese	280 g 10 oz	675 g 1 1/2 lb	2.3 kg 5 lb
ham	675 g 1 1/2 lb	1.7 kg 3 3/4 lb	5.4 kg 12 lb

Week 9

Barbecued sausages
Serve with baps and salad

YOU WILL NEED:

oil
sausages (large - e.g. 8 to 450 g (1 lb))
clear honey
Worcestershire sauce
soy sauce
tomato ketchup
oranges - juice only
white wine vinegar
garlic - crushed
paprika
salt and black pepper
chilli sauce - to taste
baps - sliced almost in half

1. Preheat the oven to 200°C/ 400°F/ gas mark 6.

2. Pour some oil to cover the base of one or two large roasting trays. Line up the sausages in the trays but do not 'overcrowd' them or it will be difficult to turn the sausages.

3. Cook the sausages in the oven, turning them over once one side has browned. When the sausages are cooked, loosen them from the base of the trays and tip off the oil. Set aside. If you have more sausages to cook repeat the above.

4. Make the barbecue sauce by mixing the honey, Worcestershire sauce, soy sauce, tomato ketchup, orange juice, vinegar and garlic together in a bowl.

Add the paprika and season to taste with the salt, black pepper and chilli sauce (use only a drop or two at first!).

5. Pile the sausages into roasting trays, pour over the sauce and toss the sausages so they are well coated. Cover

the trays with tin foil and return to the oven to re-heat the sausages and to heat the sauce.

6. Serve piping hot with two sausages in the centre of each bap.

Cook's tip

For large numbers: remember to order the baps from your supermarket and, if necessary, your sausages too.

Ingredients	Quantities for 12	Quantities for 30	Quantities for 100
oil (approx)	3 tbsp	7 tbsp	290 ml 1/2 pt
sausages	1.35 kg 3 lb	3.4 kg 7 1/2 lb	11.35 kg 25 lb
clear honey	110 g 4 oz	280 g 10 oz	900 g 2 lb
Worcestershire sauce	5 tbsp	170 ml 6 fl oz	570 ml 1 pt
soy sauce	1 1/2 tbsp	4 tbsp	200 ml 3/4 pt
tomato ketchup	4 tbsp	150 ml	425 ml 3/4 pt
oranges	1/2	1 1/2	4
white wine vinegar	1 1/2 tbsp	3 1/2 tbsp	150 ml
garlic	1 clove	2 cloves	5 cloves
paprika	pinch	1/3 tsp	1 tsp
salt & pepper	to taste	to taste	to taste
chilli sauce			
baps	12	30	100

Week 10

Pasta with ratatouille
Serve with garlic bread and salad

YOU WILL NEED:

oil
onions - peeled and sliced
garlic - crushed
green peppers - seeded and sliced
red peppers - seeded and sliced
aubergines - cut into bite-sized chunks
courgettes - cut into bite-sized chunks
tinned tomatoes
tomato purée
dried basil
salt and black pepper
sugar - to taste
pasta (see notes page 48)
oil (preferably olive oil) - to toss over
the pasta
cheddar cheese - grated

1. Heat two thirds of the oil in a large saucepan and add the onions. When they begin to soften add the garlic and the peppers. Chop the aubergines and stir them into the saucepan with the remaining oil. Add the courgettes.

2. Cook gently for 30 minutes, stirring occasionally to prevent the vegetables sticking to the bottom of the pan. Add more oil if they start to stick.

3. Add the tinned tomatoes, tomato purée and basil. Season with salt and black pepper. Bring to the boil and lower the heat and cook for a further 25-30 minutes until the vegetables are tender. Check the seasoning and stir in a little sugar if needed.

4. Cook the pasta and once it has been drained, toss generously in oil (to help prevent the pasta sticking together).

5. Serve a portion of pasta with a ladle of hot ratatouille and a sprinkle of cheese on top.

Cook's tips

If the ratatouille has too much liquid, tip a little off and add
more tomato purée. Adding more tomato purée will help
thicken the sauce and give it a shiny gloss.

For large numbers: there is a lot of chopping for this recipe so make
sure you have plenty of help! Allow longer cooking time if you are
cooking a very large quantity of ratatouille.

Ingredients	Quantities for 12	Quantities for 30	Quantities for 100
oil	150 ml 1/4 pt	425 ml 3/4 pt	1.15 lt 2 pt
onions	2 large	800 g 1 3/4 lb	2 1/2 kg 5 1/2 lb
garlic	2 cloves	5 cloves	1 head
green peppers	2 large	900 g 2 lb	3 kg 6 1/2 lb
red peppers	2 large	900 g 2 lb	3 kg 6 1/2 lb
aubergines	2 large	1.15 kg 2 1/2 lb	4 kg 9 lb
courgettes	4 large	1.35 kg 3 lb	4 1/2 kg 10 lb
tinned tomatoes	3 x 400 g 3 x 14 oz	3 x 800 g 3 x 28 oz	8 x 800 g 8 x 28 oz
tomato purée	2 large tbsp	340 g 12 oz	1.15 kg 2 1/2 lb
dried basil	1 tbsp	2 1/2 tbsp	20 g 3/4 oz
salt & pepper	to taste	to taste	to taste
sugar			
pasta	900 g 2 lb	1.8 kg 4 lb	5.9 kg 13 lb
olive oil			
cheddar cheese	225 g 8 oz	560 g 1 1/4 lb	1.8 kg 4 lb

Vegetarian

Vegetable and bean curry
Serve with rice

Serves 5 people

YOU WILL NEED:

110 g (4 oz) butter beans
(soaked overnight - maximum 12 hours - in
plenty of cold water)
2 tbsp oil
1 onion - peeled and chopped
1 level tbsp curry powder (medium strength)
2 medium carrots - peeled and cut into 5mm
(1/4 inch) slices
2 medium courgettes - cut into bit-sized chunks
2 leeks - cut into bite-sized slices
400 g (14 oz) tinned tomatoes
1 tbsp tomato purée
150 ml (1/4 pt) vegetable stock
2 tsp mixed herbs
salt and black pepper

1. Drain the beans, rinse and put them in a saucepan with enough water to cover. Bring to the boil and keep boiling for 10 minutes. Lower the heat and simmer gently for 30 minutes.

2. Heat the oil in another saucepan and add the onion. Cook slowly for 1 minute. Stir in the curry powder and cook for a further minute, stirring constantly.

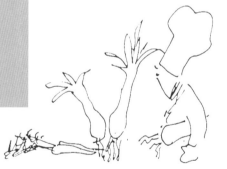

3. Add the carrots, courgettes and leeks and then stir in the tinned tomatoes, tomato purée and vegetable stock. Add the herbs and season with salt and pepper. Bring to the boil.

4. Add the drained beans and turn the heat down so the curry simmers gently for 30 minutes until all the vegetables have cooked.

5. Check the seasoning and serve with rice.

Onion and red pepper quiche

Serves 4 people

YOU WILL NEED:

Pastry

140 g (5 oz) plain flour
pinch of salt
70 g (2 1/2 oz) margarine
dried beans for baking the
pastry blind

Filling

1 tbsp oil
1 medium onion - peeled and
chopped
1 red pepper - seeded and cut into
small dice
150 ml (1/4 pt) milk
1 egg
1 egg yolk
salt and black pepper
45 g (1 1/2 oz) cheddar cheese - grated

1. Sieve the flour with the salt into a bowl. Rub the margarine in lightly until the mixture resembles coarse breadcrumbs. Add 2 tablespoons of cold water and mix with a table knife to a firm dough. It may be necessary to add more water but the pastry should not be too damp.

2. Roll out the pastry on a lightly floured surface and line a 18cm (7") flan ring. Chill for 30 minutes in the fridge. Preheat the oven to 200 C/ 400 F/ gas mark 6.

3. Prick the pastry lightly with a fork and bake blind by lining the pastry with greaseproof paper and filling it with a layer of beans. Cook the pastry in the oven for about 15 minutes, removing the paper and beans when the pastry is almost cooked (after about 10 minutes), and returning it to the oven to dry out for the final 5 minutes.

4. Heat the oil in a saucepan and cook the onion and red pepper gently until soft but not brown.

5. Mix together the milk, egg and the egg yolk in a bowl. Season with salt and black pepper.

6. Spread the vegetables over the base of the

flan case, sprinkle the cheese on top and then pour over the milk and egg mixture.

7. Return to the oven for 30 minutes or until the quiche has set and is golden brown on top.

Mushroom and tomato pizza

I am using 'packet' pizza base in this recipe as it saves time and works as well as homemade pizza dough.

Serves 4 people

YOU WILL NEED:

1 1/2 tbsp oil
1/2 onion - peeled and chopped
200 g (7 oz) tinned tomatoes
1/2 tbsp tomato purée
1/2 tsp dried oregano
salt and black pepper
110 g (4 oz) button mushrooms - sliced
1 packet (1 sachet) pizza base mix - to roll out to a circle of 20cm (8")
2 tomatoes - sliced
55 g (2 oz) cheddar cheese - grated

1. Preheat the oven to 200^{0}C/ 400^{0}F/ gas mark 6.

2. Heat half a tablespoon of oil in a saucepan and add the onion. Cook gently until soft but not coloured.

3. Add the tinned tomatoes, tomato purée and oregano. Bring to the boil and then lower the heat so the sauce simmers uncovered for about 5-10 minutes so you have a thick sauce. Season with salt and black pepper.

4. In a frying pan heat the remaining oil and add the mushrooms. Stir for a couple of minutes to cook the mushrooms and then set aside.

5. Following the instructions on the packet, make up the pizza dough with one sachet and roll out the dough into a circle (approximately 20cm (8") in diameter) onto a lightly floured surface. Place onto a greased and floured baking tray.

6. Spread the tomato sauce on top of the pizza base to within 5mm (1/4") of the edge and arrange the mushrooms and sliced tomatoes on top. Sprinkle on the cheese.

7. Cook in the oven for 25 minutes until the dough is cooked and the cheeese is golden brown on top.

Vegetable risotto

Serves 4-5 people

YOU WILL NEED:

2-3 tbsp oil
1 onion - peeled and chopped
1 green pepper - seeded and diced
2 sticks of celery - sliced finely
1 garlic clove - crushed
110 g (4 oz) button mushrooms -
trimmed and sliced
140 g (5 oz) long grain rice
400 g (14 oz) tinned tomatoes
200 ml (7 fl oz) vegetable stock
1 tsp dried mixed herbs
salt and black pepper
30 g (1 oz) parmesan cheese - grated

1. Heat the oil in a saucepan and add the onion, green pepper and celery. Cook gently until the vegetables are soft but not coloured. Stir in the garlic and mushrooms and cook for a further couple of minutes.

2. Stir in the rice and then add the tinned tomatoes, vegetable stock and herbs. Season with salt and black pepper. Bring to the boil and lower the heat so the rice mixture simmers gently for about 12 minutes until the rice is cooked. Add more stock if it is looking rather dry. Remove from the heat.

3. Adjust the seasoning and stir in the parmesan cheese.

Courgette and aubergine lasagne

Serves 5 people

YOU WILL NEED:

1 tbsp oil
1 onion - peeled and chopped
1 garlic clove - crushed
800 g (28 oz) tinned tomatoes
1 tbsp tomato purée
1 tsp mixed herbs
salt and black pepper
2 medium courgettes
1 large aubergine
6tbsp olive oil
1110 g (4 oz) lasagne (no pre-cooking needed)
70 g (2½ oz) cheddar cheese - grated

1. Preheat the grill and set the oven to 190°C/ 350°F/ gas mark 4.

2. Heat the oil in a saucepan and add the onions. Cook gently until soft but not coloured and then stir in the garlic.

3. Add the tinned tomatoes, tomato purée and herbs. Season with salt and black pepper. Bring to the boil, then lower the heat so the sauce simmers uncovered for 30 minutes by which time the sauce will have thickened (you may need to break up the tomatoes with a wooden spoon). Check the seasoning.

4. Slice the courgettes and aubergines lengthways, trimming off the ends. Using a pastry brush, brush one side with olive oil. Place the slices under the grill (oiled side up) until they are beginning to brown. Turn over, brush with olive oil and return under the grill to brown.

5. Layer up into a pie dish, starting with the sauce, followed by the vegetables and finally the lasagne. Repeat the layering up in the same order, finishing with the remaining sauce on top, having left enough to generously cover the lasagne. Sprinkle over the cheese.

6. Place in the oven for about 30 minutes until the lasagne is cooked and the surface is golden brown and bubbling.

Stuffed green peppers

Serves 4 people

2 tbsp oil
1 small onion - peeled and chopped
1 large carrot - peeled and chopped
finely
110 g (4 oz) button mushrooms -
trimmed and sliced finely
70 g (2 1/2 oz) long grain rice - cooked
(see notes page 49)
55 g (2 oz) walnuts - chopped
55 g (2 oz) cheddar cheese - grated
salt and black pepper
2 large green peppers - halved and
seeded

1. Preheat the oven to 180°C/ 350°F/ gas mark 4.

2. Heat the oil in the saucepan and cook the onion and carrot gently until soft but not coloured. Add the mushrooms and cook stirring for a further couple of minutes.

3. In a bowl mix the cooked vegetables, cooked rice, walnuts and half the cheese together. Season with salt and pepper.

4. Place the pepper halves onto a greased baking tray. Pile the rice mixture into the halves and pat down. Sprinkle the remaining cheese on top.

5. Cook in the oven for 20-25 minutes until the peppers are cooked.

Salad, hot breads and
hints on cooking pasta and rice

Salad - approximate quantities

1 large iceburg lettuce feeds 15 people
1 cucumber feeds 20 people
450 g (1 lb) of tomatoes feeds 18 people
1 punnet of salad cress feeds 12-20 people

Vinaigrette

Makes approximately 570 ml (1 pt)

1 rounded tsp Dijon mustard
1 garlic clove - crushed
1/4 lemon - juice only
2 tsp sugar
salt and black pepper
85 ml (3 fl oz) white wine vinegar
425 ml (3/4 pt) oil

1. Put the mustard, garlic, lemon juice, sugar, salt, black pepper and then the vinegar into a bowl and mix together using a balloon whisk.

2. Pour the oil in a steady stream into the mixture, whisking all the time. Adjust the seasonings if necessary.

Garlic bread

15 portions

55 g (2 oz) margarine
55 g (2 oz) butter
2 garlic cloves - crushed
salt and black pepper

1 large french stick

1. Preheat the oven to 200°C/400°F/gas mark 6.

2. Beat all the ingredients together well.

3. Slice the french stick in half lengthways (not all the way through) and spread the garlic butter generously on one side. Any left over butter can be used by spreading it on the other side.

4. Cut the french stick across into slices (all the way through) and then wrap it well in the foil.

5. Put the garlic bread in the oven for about 20-25 minutes.

Herbed bread

15 portions

55 g (2 oz) margarine
55 g (2 oz) butter
2 tbsp chopped fresh mixed herbs -
parsley, thyme, rosemary, chives, etc
salt and black pepper

1 large french stick

Follow the recipe as for garlic bread.

You can use dried mixed herbs but they are not as good as fresh herbs.

Cooking Pasta

I find the best pasta to use when cooking is 'penne rigate' or 'rigatoni'. It is easy and does not tend to break up like other types of pasta.

Pasta needs as much 'space' as possible to cook in, so make sure you have plenty of salted water (be generous with the salt), in a large saucepan.

Once the water has boiled, add a little oil to the water (to help prevent the pasta from sticking together) and then add the pasta. When the water has come back to the boil, lower the heat to simmer. By keeping the saucepan lid off you will find that the water will not boil over while the pasta is cooking! Follow the cooking instructions recommended on the packet of pasta (usually 10-12 minutes). To check the pasta is cooked take a piece out and it should be 'al dente', firm to the bite, not too hard or soft. Drain the pasta through a colander and tip it back into the saucepan.

If the pasta is not going to be mixed with the sauce, stir in a generous amount of oil (preferably olive oil) as this will help prevent the pasta sticking together. If you are cooking an enormous amount of pasta it is inevitable that it will start sticking together at some point.

Cooking rice

Make sure the rice you are using is 'easy cook' long grain rice. (I use 'Uncle Ben's').

As a general rule, for every 450g (1lb) of rice you are cooking use 1.15lt (2pt) of salted water (be generous with the salt). If you are cooking a large quantity you will not need quite as much as this. As a guide, for every 340g (12oz) use 570ml (1pt).

Once you have boiled the water, add the rice but do not stir as it may then start sticking together. Bring back to the boil and then lower the heat so the rice cooks gently. You will find that the rice will absorb all the water by the time it is cooked (about 10-12 minutes, allow a little longer for a large amount). To check that the rice is cooked, take a piece out and it should be 'al dente' like the pasta, firm to the bite but not too hard or soft. (You may need to drain the rice through a sieve if the water has not been totally absorbed.)

If you are not serving the rice immediately it will keep its heat on top of the stove in the saucepan with the lid on.

Section 3: Alpha Supper Parties

Many Alpha course leaders like to hold an 'end-of-term' supper party to which participants can invite friends and family.

As well as providing a chance for participants to let their hair down, these dinners are a great chance to recruit for future Alpha courses! It's important therefore to make the evening special and the food is a vital part of that.

At the Alpha supper parties I cater for, we always try to have tablecloths (even if they are paper) on the tables, candles, 'proper' cutlery, plates and glasses and even a flower arrangement or two! For those who think that church catering is just tea and biscuits, it is a nice surprise and helps to set the tone for the evening. Generally, people bring a bottle of wine (don't forget the corkscrews!) or you can serve a fruit punch if appropriate. Make sure there is plenty of cold water on the tables.

In this book I have suggested two supper party menus, one for winter and one for summer, together with a vegetarian alternative. As presentation is important, I have included a few tips, as well as revealing for the first time in print the secret of Harriet's Fruit Punch!

Party Menu 1
Winter

Memsahib's party chicken
Spiced yellow rice
Mixed leaf salad
Chocolate roulade

Party Menu 2
Summer

Chicken with lemon and tarragon
Spiced yellow rice/ New potatoes tossed in mint
Mixed leaf salad
Fresh fruit pavlova

Vegetarian

Leek and roquefort torte

Party Menu 1

The Memsahib's party chicken

"On my first journey to India with two friends I was designated as the tour leader, otherwise known as memsahib. So many things can go wrong while travelling in India that the responsibility of making daily decisions is a heavy one. My heart used to sink when my friends asked, "Well then, what are memsahib's plans for today?" The following recipe is for a memsahib who is too busy to cook elaborately but who wants to please her friends with something more exciting than coronation chicken.

Coating pieces of cold chicken with a spicy sauce is easy and effective. It goes well with bread or new potaotes and a green salad and is easily made in large quantities."

Sainsbury's Book of Parties by Josceline Dimbleby
Websters International Publishers

Serves 24 people

4 x 1 3/4 - 2 kg (3 1/2 - 4 lb) fresh roasting chickens
10 - 12 tbsp mayonnaise
1 kg (2 lb) Greek yoghurt
4 tbsp tomato purée
6 - 8 tbsp tikka paste
2 large bunches fresh coriander
1 large bunch of parsley
salt and black pepper

1. Roast the chickens beforehand in a preheated oven at 200°C/400°F/ gas mark 6 for 1 - 1 1/2 hours and leave until cold.

2. Carve the breasts of the chickens into smallish pieces and then pick all the flesh you can get off the rest of the chickens.

3. Put the mayonnaise, yoghurt and tomato purée in a large bowl. Mix together and stir in the tikka paste to taste, adding salt and black pepper if you feel the mixture needs it.

4. Save some of the best sprigs of big leaves of the coriander for decoration and then pull the rest of the leaves off the stems and chop roughly. Chop the parsley finely. Stir the chopped coriander leaves and parsley into the yoghurt mixture.

5. Add the chicken pieces to the mixture and stir with a wooden spoon so the chicken is thoroughly coated.

6. Cover the bowl loosely with cling film and refrigerate until needed.

7. Serve in large shallow serving dishes and decorate with whole coriander leaves.

Cook's tip

Josceline roasts the chickens in this recipe but I poach mine. If you would prefer to poach them, please see cooking instructions in the recipe for 'Chicken with lemon and tarragon'.

Party Menu 2

Chicken with lemon and tarragon

Serves 24 people

4 x 1.6 - 1.8 kg (3½ - 4 lb) chickens
4 onions - peeled and roughly chopped
4 carrots - roughly chopped
4 sticks of celery - roughly chopped
8 sprigs of parsley
4 bay leaves
1tsp black peppercorns

Sauce

1 lt (1¾ pt) mayonnaise - use a brand of
mayonnaise with a mild flavour
900 g (2 lb) Greek yoghurt
4 lemons - rind and juice
110 g (4 oz) fresh tarragon - remove tough
stalks and chop the leaves
salt, black pepper and sugar to taste
bunch of watercress to decorate

1. Put the chickens into large saucepans and divide the chopped vegetables, parsley, bay leaves and peppercorns between the saucepans. Fill the saucepans with enough cold water to cover the chickens and place the lids on top.

2. Bring to the boil, then lower the heat and poach for 1 ¼ - 1 ½ hours until the chickens are cooked - the drumsticks should feel loose and wobbly. Remove the chickens from the saucepans and allow to cool.

3. Skin the chickens, remove the flesh from the bones and break into smallish pieces.

4. Mix all the ingredients for the sauce together in a large bowl and season with salt, black pepper and sugar to taste. Stir in the cold chicken pieces. Cover loosely with cling film and chill until needed.

5. Serve in large shallow serving dishes, piling up the chicken in the middle and decorate with the watercress.

Cook's tips

It is easier to remove the flesh from the bones while the chicken is still warm, but allow the chicken to go cold properly before mixing with the sauce.

I prefer to make this with home made mayonnaise using equal quantities of sunflower and olive oil, but supermarket mayonnaise is perfectly adequate. The leftover egg whites can be used to make pavlovas.

Do not use dried tarragon - it does not achieve the same result.

For large numbers: you could use chicken breasts instead of whole chickens if you have a lot of people to cook for and you want to save time, but make sure that your budget stretches to this.

Vegetarian

Leek and roquefort torte
A vegetarian alternative to the chicken dishes

Serves 8 people

225 g (8 ox) plain flour
pinch of salt and cayenne
55 g (2 oz) lard
55 g (2 oz) margarine
*55 g (2 oz) cheddar cheese - finely grated (*optional)
dried beans for baking the pastry blind

Filling

3 tbsp olive oil
900 g (2 lb) leeks - trimmed and chopped finely
225 g (8 oz) cream cheese (full fat)
2 eggs
110 g (4 oz) roquefort cheese - grated
salt and black pepper
45 g (1 1/2 oz) parmesan cheese - grated

1. Sieve the flour with the salt and cayenne into a bowl. Rub the lard and margarine in lightly until the mixture resembles coarse breadcrumbs, then stir in the cheese. Add 3 - 4 tablespoons of cold water and mix with a table knife to a firm dough. It may be necessary to add more water but the pastry should not be too damp.

2. Roll out the pastry on a lightly floured surface and line a 25cm (10") flan ring. Chill for 30 minutes in the fridge. Preheat the oven to 200^{0}C/ 400^{0}F/ gas mark 6.

3. Prick the pastry lightly with a fork and bake blind by lining the pastry with greaseproof paper and filling it with a layer of dried beans. Cook the pastry in the oven for about 20 minutes, removing the paper and beans when the pastry is almost cooked (after 10 - 15 minutes) and returning it to the oven to dry out for the final 5 minutes.

4. Lower the oven to 180^{0}C/ 350^{0}F/ gas mark 4.

5. Heat the oil in a sauecepan and add the leeks. Cook gently until soft. Remove from the heat, drain off any liquid and allow to cool gently.

6. Mix together the cream cheese, eggs and roquefort in a bowl and then stir in the leeks. Season with salt and black pepper.

7. Pour the mixture into the pastry case and sprinkle over parmesan. Put the torte into the oven and cook for about 35 minutes. The filling should be set and golden brown on top.

Rice and salad

Spiced yellow rice

Serves 24 people

1.15 kg (2 1/2 lb) long grain rice
(see notes page 49)
1 level tbsp salt
2 tsp ground tumeric
3 x 2cm (1") sticks of cinammon
10 whole cloves
chopped parsley to decorate

1. Bring 2 lt (3 1/2 pt) water in a saucepan to the boil.

2. Mix together the rice, salt and tumeric in a bowl and add the cinammon and cloves. Pour the rice mixture into the boiling water.

3. Once the water has come back to the boil, lower the heat so the rice cooks gently. Cook for 10 - 12 minutes until the rice is 'al dente' to the bite, not too hard or soft. Remove from the heat. All the water will have been absorbed by the rice.

4. Serve in a large dish decorated with chopped parsley.

Cook's tip

For large numbers: if you are cooking more rice remember not to use quite so much water (see notes on cooking rice page 49).

New potatoes

An alternative to spiced yellow rice is to cook new potatoes which are popular in the summer. Allow 110g (4oz) of new potatoes per person and once cooked, toss generously in butter and chopped mint.

Mixed leaf salad

Serves 24 people

Mixture of 3-4 lettuces (e.g. oak leaf, curly endive, lollo rosso, iceberg)
225 g (8 oz) french beans - topped and tailed
1/2 cucumber - sliced
675 g (1½ lb) cherry tomatoes - cut in half
vinaigrette (see recipe on page 46)
chopped parsley to decorate

1. Wash and dry the salad leaves and break gently into small pieces.

2. Bring a saucepan of salted water to the boil and put the french beans into the water. Bring back to the boil, lower the heat and cook the beans for 2 minutes then drain them. Run under cold water until the beans are cold.

3. Mix the salad leaves with the french beans, cucumber and tomatoes in a large bowl. Toss over the vinaigrette just before serving and decorate with the chopped parsley.

Cook's tip

You could make a more interesting salad by the addition of blanched sugar snap peas or mange toutes, croutons, fried diced bacon, pumpkin seeds or flakes of parmesan.

Puddings

Chocolate roulade

Assuming your mixer is a domestic one, you will need to make this recipe in two halves as your mixer will not be able to cope with the number of eggs it has to whisk all at once.

Serves 24 people

795 g (1¾lb) dark chocolate - broken into smallish pieces
1 tbsp instant coffee
290 ml (½ pt) water
18 eggs
510 g (1 lb 2 oz) caster sugar
1 lt (1 ¾ pt) double cream
icing sugar to decorate
bakewell paper

1. Preheat the oven to 200°C/ 400°F/ gas mark 6. Line 2 large baking trays with bakewell paper making sure that the paper goes 4cm (1 ½") up the sides.

2. Put the chocolate, coffee and water into a bowl and sit the bowl over a saucepan of almost simmering water (the bowl should not touch the water) until the chocolate has melted.

3. Meanwhile separate the eggs and beat the yolks with the sugar until pale and mousse-like. It should be thick enough to leave a trail on top of the mixture when the whisk is lifted. Stir in the chocolate.

4. Whisk the egg whites in a clean bowl until stiff (but not dry) peaks start to form. Stir a large spoonful of egg white into the chocolate mixture, then carefully fold in the remainder with a large metal spoon (do not 'over work' the mixture).

5. Pour the mixture into the prepared trays and bake them in the oven for 12 - 15 minutes until firm to the touch. Once cooked, place a damp tea towel over the top to help prevent the roulades from drying out and allow to cool.

6. On a work surface put a layer of bakewell paper, larger than the roulade, on top of a larger sheet of tin foil. Turn out the roulade on to this and peel off the paper. Repeat this for the other roulade.

7. Whip the cream and spread it evenly over each roulade. Then roll up lengthways like a swiss roll starting with the far end and pulling the tin foil and paper towards you to help roll it up. Allow to chill for several hours before serving.

8. Dust with sieved icing sugar and serve sliced into 24 slices.

Cook's tips

You can use greaseproof paper instead of bakewell paper, but you will need to brush the paper with oil and sprinkle with plain flour and then caster sugar when preparing the trays.

When you come to slicing the roulade keep a jug of very hot water beside you and as you cut dip a sharp knife into the water and dry it. You will find it much easier to cut the roulade.

Fresh fruit pavlova

Assuming your food mixer is a domestic one, you will need to make this recipe in two halves as your mixer will not be able to cope with the number of egg whites it has to whisk all at once.

Serves 24 people

12 egg whites
675 g (1 1/2 lb) caster sugar
1 tbsp cornflour
1 tbsp vanilla essence
1 tbsp white wine vinegar
*1.15 lt (2 pt) double cream
1.35 kg (3 lb) mixed prepared fruits e.g.
strawberries, raspberries, blueberries,
peaches, nectarines, kiwi fruit, pineapple

1. Preheat the oven to 140°C/ 275°F/ gas mark 1. Put a sheet of bakewell paper onto each of two baking trays.

2. Whisk the egg whites on the fastest speed of your machine until stiff peaks form (do not over whisk). Immediately pour the sugar in a continuous, fast stream keeping the machine whisking fast and then stop.

3. Carefully fold in the cornflour, vanilla essence and vinegar with a large metal spoon.

4. Spoon the mixture onto the baking trays into two to four 'nest' shapes.

5. Place in the oven for about an hour. They should be a pale brown colour on the outside and soft inside. Allow to go cold, then peel off the paper carefully from the pavlova.

6. Whip the cream and divide it between each pavlova. Arrange your fruit on top.

*If you are making two pavlovas from this recipe you will only need 850 ml (1 1/2 pt) double cream.

Drink

Harriet's fruit punch

Makes approximately 60-70 wine glasses

3 lt orange juice - chilled
3 lt pineapple juice - chilled
2 lt ginger ale - chilled
1 1/2 lt lemonade - chilled
a few drops of angostura bitters
5 large oranges - cut into half and sliced
340 g (12 oz) strawberries - husks removed and sliced
1 bunch of mint

1. About 20 minutes before serving make up the punch. Mix together the orange and pineapple juices, ginger ale and lemonade.

2. Stir in the angostura bitters, the fruit and the sprigs of mint.

Cook's tips

Do not make the punch more than 20 minutes before needed as it will lose its 'fizz'.

If you are unable to chill the drink, make sure you have plenty of ice to stir into the punch once it has been made up.

About the author

Harriet Lanyon trained at Leith's before coming, via catering jobs at home and abroad, to start her own business 'Harriet' in 1990.

Weddings, cocktail parties, business and private lunches and dinners account for most of her work, but her reputation for making a meal for 300 taste just as good as a dinner for two has made her a popular choice with those who have many to feed, but only a limited budget.

Coaxed into cooking for Alpha for one week of a 100 person Alpha course at Holy Trinity Brompton in 1991, she became HTB's regular Alpha cook until 1994, feeding more than 20,000 mouths in the process!

Acknowledgements

To Anna Garnier, Pat Reid and Sherolyn Tramel for 'lending' me recipes. To my husband Robert for eating most of these recipes many times over.